easynoodles

easynoodles

recipes from China, Japan and South-east Asia

RYLAND
PETERS
& SMALL
LONDON NEW YORK

Kimiko Barber

photography by William Lingwood

First published in Great Britain in 2003
by Ryland Peters & Small
Kirkman House, 12–14 Whitfield Street,
London W1T 2RP
www.rylandpeters.com

10 9 8 7 6 5 4 3 2 1

ISBN 1 84172 385 1

A catalogue record for this book is available from
the British Library.

Printed in China

Designer Luis Peral-Aranda
Commissioning Editor Elsa Petersen-Schepelern
Production Deborah Wehner
Art Director Gabriella Le Grazie
Publishing Director Alison Starling

Food Stylist Joss Herd
Stylist Liz Belton

Notes

All spoon measurements are level unless
otherwise specified.

Uncooked or partly cooked eggs should not be
served to the very young, the very old or frail, or
to pregnant women.

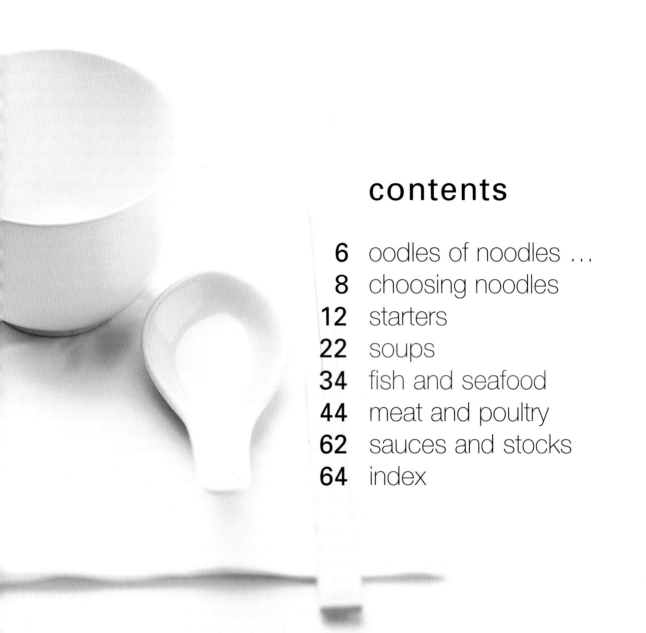

contents

oodles of noodles ...

Noodles are the 'fast food' of Asia – they are quick, instantly satisfying, healthy and wholesome to eat. It is because Asian noodles are made from many different varieties of starch – unlike Italian pasta, which is made of wheat flour – that they offer almost infinite combinations of texture, flavour and taste.

Anyone who has travelled across the Asian continent will have seen the ramshackle noodle stands along dusty roads in China; bustling noodle bars around Tokyo's busiest railway stations; international bankers slurping noodles while keeping a weary eye on Hong Kong's Hang Seng index, their mobile phones tucked into their shoulders; noodle vendors' tiny boats gently paddling through Bangkok's floating markets; Singapore's narrow streets blocked by itinerant food hawkers' plastic tables and chairs; or the tempting smells of noodle-pedlars wafting past sunbathers on the endless beaches of Bali. Noodles are central to Asian food culture.

Choosing noodles

Asian ingredients, once considered strange and difficult to obtain, have become much more widely available, not just from specialist Asian shops but also in supermarkets. Although I have my own reservations about the ever-increasing dependency on supermarkets, I recognize their success in broadening culinary horizons. I can now prepare a gourmet lunch for two in 10 minutes or less.

Wheat Noodles

Wheat noodles are the oldest type of noodles. They were originally from northern China, where the climate is more suited to wheat cultivation, but now are also produced in Japan. As with Italian pasta, some are made with egg in the dough, and others not. Noodles made without egg are always white in colour: those made with egg are yellowish. They are made in a variety of shapes and thicknesses, available both dry and fresh.

Cooking instructions are given for dried noodles, and also for fresh, when they are available in that form. The Japanese noodle cooking method deserves special mention (below).

The general rule in choosing the right noodle is to use thinner ones for refined soups, whereas the thicker varieties can stand up to more robust flavours.

Japanese noodle cooking method

All dried Japanese noodles should be cooked in the same way. Bring a saucepan of water to the boil, add the noodles and return to the boil. Skim with a slotted spoon, then add a splash of cold water, return to the boil, then skim again. Repeat 2–3 times. When cooked, rinse to remove excess starch and reheat by dipping in boiling water.

Japanese Udon Noodles

Originating in the Sanuki region of Shikoku Island, udon noodles are made in round, square or flat shapes. Usually served hot in dashi broth but can also be served stir-fried or chilled. Available fresh in vacuum packs, or in dried form.

Fresh: rinse in warm water and boil for 1 minute

Dried: boil for 3–5 minutes (see boxed text, left)

Japanese Somen Noodles

Udon and soba noodles are seen as the everyday food of the Japanese working man. Somen, on the other hand, are elegant, thin and white, considered to be more refined and therefore at home in Buddhist temples. They are traditionally served cold with a simple dashi-based dipping sauce. When sold dry, they are often tied with ribbons in neat bundles.

Dried: boil for about 3 minutes (see boxed text, left)

Japanese Ramen Egg Noodles

Ramen noodles are not Japanese, but the Japanese idea of Chinese wheat noodles. They are usually rather crinkled and pale yellow; either dried or fresh. Vacuum packed Chinese egg noodles make a perfect substitute.

Fresh: rinse in warm water and boil for 2 minutes

Dried: boil for about 3–5 minutes (see boxed text, left)

Chinese Wheat Noodles

Often sold in 'nests', with one nest making 1 serving.

Fresh: rinse in warm water, boil for 2–3 minutes

Dried: boil for 3–5 minutes

Chinese Thin Yellow Egg Noodles

Fresh: rinse in warm water, boil for 2 minutes

Dried: boil for 3–5 minutes

Chinese Thick Yellow Egg Noodles

Fresh: rinse in warm water, boil for 3 minutes

Dried: boil for 8 minutes

Shanghai Noodles

These noodles can be made from wheat alone, or from a wheat and egg dough.
Similar to Japanese ramen.

Fresh: rinse in warm water and boil for 2 minutes

Dried: boil for about 3 minutes (see method left)

Hokkien Noodles

Thick pale yellow noodles, originally from the Hokkien province of China but nowadays travel the globe on a Malaysian passport. They are widely used for stir-fry dishes and can be substituted for Shanghai noodles or Peking noodles.

Fresh: rinse in warm water and boil for 2 minutes

Dried: boil for about 3 minutes (see method left)

Chinese Wonton Wrappers or Skins, and Dumpling Wrappers, Spring Roll Wrappers, Philippine Lumpia Wrappers

Made from wheat and egg noodle dough. Available fresh or frozen in packs of 175–225 g, usually 7.5 cm square.

Always fresh or frozen: sold in refrigerated section. If frozen, let thaw. If filling, add filling, seal, then boil for 4–5 minutes, or deep-fry for 1 minute These wrappers are sold in packs of 50–100 in various sizes. Leftover fresh wrappers may be resealed and frozen for future use.

Rice Noodles

In those parts of China and South-east Asia where wheat isn't grown, rice starch or rice flour is used to make noodles. They are made in thicknesses ranging from the finest hair-thin vermicelli to wide flat ribbons, and are available fresh or dried. Vietnamese ricepaper wrappers are also made from rice flour. Used for soups, stir-frying or deep-frying. They are extremely versatile. If unavailable, beanthread noodles make a good substitute.

Fine Rice Vermicelli Noodles (*banh hoi*)

Fresh: rinse in hot water, then cook for 1 minute

Dried: soak in hot water for 15 minutes and boil for 1 minute or deep-fry for 30 seconds

Thin Rice Vermicelli Noodles (*bun*)

Used in soups and spring rolls. Sold in large packets, or in small bundles of about 30 g each, suitable for 1 serving.

Fresh: rinse in hot water, then cook for 1 minute

Dried: boil for 1–2 minutes

Rice Ribbon Noodles (*ho fun*)

When fresh, often sold in folded sheets, like a small book. Sometimes uncut, so cut into wide strips before use. Can be used for Vietnamese pho noodle soups.

Fresh: rinse in hot water, then cook for 1 minute

Dried: soak in hot (not boiling) water for 15 minutes, then boil for 1 minute, or stir-fry for 1 minute. May also be deep-fried.

Rice Sticks

It can be confusing as Chinese sometimes call rice vermicelli rice sticks. These flat dried noodles made of rice flour and water are available in three main sizes. Thin ones are usually used in soups while medium, the most popular, are served in soups, stir-fries and salads. The wider versions are usually used in Thai dishes. Fresh rice sticks are called rice sheet noodles and are sold in either pre-sliced or in whole sheet form.

Fresh: rinse in cold water, then cook for 1 minute

Dried: soak in hot (not boiling) water for 15 minutes, then boil for 1 minute, or stir-fry for 1 minute. May also be deep-fried.

Ricepaper Sheets

Dry, very brittle translucent sheets made of rice flour. Round or triangular in shape, they usually have a patterned surface – the imprint of the bamboo trays on which they are dried.

Always dried: dip into a shallow bowl of warm water until softened (just a few seconds). Put onto a plate or work surface, add filling, then roll up and serve. Do not work on a wood surface, or the sheets will dry out again. Can also be deep-fried until crisp. Sold in packs of 50 large or 100 small. Leftovers may be wrapped in 2 layers of clingfilm and sealed well.

Beanthread Noodles

Made from mung bean flour, this family of noodles is also known as cellophane noodles or glass noodles, and include Japanese harusame ('spring rain') noodles.

Almost colourless, these dried noodles are sold in bundles of various sizes. For easier handling, I recommend buying smaller sizes. Common are the 30 g bundles, perfect for 1 serving.

Chinese Beanthread Noodles

Available in various thicknesses

Dried: soak in hot (not boiling) water for 15 minutes, then drain and boil or stir-fry for 1 minute

Japanese Harusame Noodles

Harusame means 'spring rain' in Japanese, and as the name implies, these noodles are thin, delicate, semi-transparent and white. Traditionally they are used in soups and salads. They have a slightly chewier texture and are interchangeable with shirataki noodles.

Fresh: as for shirataki noodles

Dried: deep-fry until white and puffy – about 30 seconds

Buckwheat Noodles

Usually made from a combination of buckwheat and wheat flour, and sometimes also yam potato starch. They are slightly flecked and usually mushroom coloured, they are sold in dried form outside Japan. Elegantly coloured green tea noodles (cha-soba) contain ground green tea leaves.

Japanese Soba Noodles

Usually made from a combination of buckwheat and wheat flour, and sometimes also yam potato starch.

They are used in soup or served chilled with dipping sauce. They represent the epitome of noodles in Tokyo, while udons are the noodles of the Osaka region.

Fresh: boil for 2 minutes

Dried: boil for 4 minutes (see boxed text, page 8)

Korean Naeng Myun Noodles

The Korean version of Japanese soba noodles are chewier and paler in colour. They are made from a mixture of buckwheat flour, potato starch and cornstarch. In Korean, the name means 'cold noodle' – the most popular way of serving them. If difficult to find, soba noodles are a good substitute.

Fresh: boil for 3 minutes

Dried: boil for 5 minutes

Potato Starch Noodles

Also made from the starch of the yam potato (not related to regular potatoes).

Japanese Shirataki Noodles

Not strictly noodles, but fine strands of *konnyaku*, a jelly-like block made from the starch of the yam potato, also known as devil's tongue plant. The noodles are often associated with sukiyaki, the Japanese table-cooked dish of beef and vegetables (page 53).

Always fresh: usually sold floating in water in clear, giant, sausage-shaped plastic packets. Harusame noodles are a good substitute.

Korean Dang Myun Noodles

Tougher, stronger and longer than the Japanese variety, they are resilient and chewy and have the ability to soak up flavours without becoming soggy. Used in jap chae (page 54). If unavailable, beanthread vermicelli noodles make a lighter, less substantial substitute.

Always dried: soak in boiling water for 10 minutes, then drain and stir-fry for 1 minute.

steamed pork noodle dumplings

3 dried shiitake mushrooms

500 g minced pork

4 spring onions, finely chopped

2 garlic cloves, finely crushed

3 cm fresh ginger,
peeled and grated

70 g dry breadcrumbs

2 tablespoons soy sauce

2 tablespoons hoisin sauce

1 egg, beaten

a small bunch of fresh coriander,
finely chopped

500 g fresh thin wheat or egg
noodles, or Peking noodles*

500 g bok choy,
coarsely chopped

Chilli Dipping Sauce or
Sweet Chilli Dipping Sauce
(pages 62–63), to serve

a bamboo steamer

Serves 6–8

*If using dried noodles, soak for
5 minutes in hot water, then boil
for 1–2 minutes.*

Put the shiitake mushrooms into a small bowl, cover with boiling water and let soak for 10 minutes. Drain. Discard the stems and finely chop the caps.

Put the mushrooms, pork, spring onions, garlic, ginger, breadcrumbs, soy sauce, hoisin sauce, egg and coriander leaves into a large bowl and mix thoroughly. Cover and let stand in the refrigerator for at least 30 minutes to develop the flavours.

Take 1 tablespoon of the mixture and roll between your palms to make a ball. Repeat until all the mixture has been used.

Hold 4–5 strands of noodles in your hand and wrap around the ball, finishing with the noodle ends underneath. Repeat with the remaining balls.

Line the bamboo steaming basket with the bok choy and arrange the wrapped balls, in a single layer, leaving a 2 cm gap between each ball. Cover and set the steamer over a wok or saucepan of simmering water. Steam them for 8–12 minutes or until the dumplings are cooked – the noodles will become glossy when ready.

Transfer the steamed bok choy and dumplings to a platter and serve with a dipping sauce. Alternatively, the dumplings may be served in the steamers.

Variation You may also use thin dried rice noodles – soak them in hot water for 10 minutes before using.

starters

sang choy bow
lettuce boats with pork noodles

50 g dried rice vermicelli noodles

3 tablespoons peanut oil

2 garlic cloves, crushed

3 cm fresh ginger, peeled and finely chopped

200 g minced pork and veal, mixed half and half

100 g canned bamboo shoots, rinsed, drained and finely chopped

6 canned water chestnuts, rinsed, drained and finely chopped

1 tablespoon soy sauce

1 tablespoon hoisin sauce

4 spring onions, finely chopped, plus extra to serve

sea salt and freshly ground black pepper

To serve

16 baby cos lettuce leaves, such as Little Gem

2 red chillies, finely chopped (optional)

Spicy Soy Vinaigrette Dip (page 63)

Makes 16

This favourite Chinese restaurant dish is easy to make at home. It is usually made with meat only, but extra rice vermicelli noodles will lighten the mixture and give it more texture. I like to use baby cos lettuce leaves instead of the traditional iceberg lettuce. It's also a very sociable dish – prepare all the elements and let your guests make up their own parcels.

Put the noodles into a large bowl and cover with boiling water. Let stand for 5 minutes or until the noodles have softened. Drain, rinse under cold running water and drain as much water you can get out by gently squeezing them with your hand. Cut them into 3 cm lengths with scissors.

Heat the oil in a wok or large frying pan and swirl to coat. Add the garlic, ginger and minced meat and stir-fry over high heat until the meat is well browned, 1–2 minutes.

Reduce the heat to medium and add the bamboo shoots and water chestnuts. Season with soy sauce, hoisin sauce, salt and pepper.

Turn off the heat, add the noodles and chopped spring onions and mix well. (You may prepare up to this point 3 hours in advance.)

Divide the meat mixture into 16 equal portions and spoon each portion into a lettuce leaf. Garnish with chopped spring onions. Serve with a dish of chopped red chilli and Spicy Soy Vinaigrette Dip for those who prefer to turn up the heat.

This dish brings back memories of summer evenings when I was a child in Japan. After bathing and changing into a crisp *yukata* (cotton or linen kimono), we would sit on bamboo benches in the garden listening to the chimes of a wind bell and the song of crickets. My grandmother served the white noodles floating in a big lacquered tub of iced water.

chilled somen noodles
with wasabi and dipping sauce

about 400 g dried somen noodles
(75 g per person as a starter,
100 g as a main course)

Soy dipping sauce

8 dried shiitake mushrooms

250 ml Dashi (page 62)

125 ml mirin (sweetened
Japanese rice wine)
or dry sherry

60 ml soy sauce

To serve

3 cm fresh ginger,
peeled and finely grated

1 sheet dried nori seaweed,
thinly sliced

8 spring onions, finely
chopped diagonally

1 baby cucumber,
peeled and thinly sliced

8 cooked prawns,
peeled, but with tail fins intact

Serves 4–6

Put the shiitake mushrooms into a bowl and cover with hot water. Leave to rehydrate for at least 15 minutes or until softened. Drain, reserving the soaking liquid. Cut off and discard the hard stems and thinly slice the caps.

Put the dashi into a saucepan and heat gently until almost boiling. Reduce the heat immediately, add the mirin and soy sauce and return to the boil. Turn off the heat and let cool to room temperature. You may prepare up to this point the day before and refrigerate until ready to use.

Bring a large saucepan of water to the boil and add the noodles, one bundle at a time. Stir with chopsticks each time you add a bundle to make sure they separate. Watch the saucepan carefully and stand by with a glass of cold water ready.

When the water begins to boil over, add the cold water. This is called *bikkuri mizu* ('surprise water') and it is used to make the outside and inside of the noodles cook at the same speed. Return to the boil and turn off the heat. Drain and rinse the noodles under cold running water, drain again and chill.

To serve, float the noodles in a large glass bowl or separate small bowls, filled with ice and water. Put the ginger, seaweed, spring onions, cucumber and prawns on a separate plate and put the soy dipping sauce in a bowl. Guests choose their own combinations.

lobster noodle salad
with coconut and fruit

An exotic salad I found on a holiday in South-east Asia. Fresh coconuts aren't always available, but if you see them for sale in your market, buy one and try this salad. The kind you need is the brown hairy type.

200 g dried beanthread noodles

2 medium cooked lobsters

2 fresh coconuts

Dressing

1 tablespoon palm sugar or soft brown sugar

freshly squeezed juice of 4 limes

1 teaspoon freshly ground green pepper

1/2 teaspoon salt

2 tablespoons peanut oil

To serve

1 fresh starfruit, thinly sliced

25 g fresh coriander leaves, coarsely chopped

25 g fresh mint leaves, coarsely chopped

2 tablespoons roasted peanuts, coarsely chopped, plus extra to serve (optional)

Serves 4

Put the noodles into a bowl, cover with very hot water and let soak for 10 minutes or until soft. Drain, rinse under cold running water and drain again. Chop into 5 cm lengths with scissors and set aside.

Remove the flesh from the cooked lobsters and shred it finely.

Crack open the coconuts and scoop out the white flesh. Using a fork, shred the coconut flesh into small strips.

Put the dressing ingredients into a bowl and stir well to dissolve the sugar.

Put the noodles into a large bowl, add the lobster and coconut, pour the dressing over the top and stir gently.

Transfer to a large serving dish, arrange the starfruit slices on top, then add the coriander, mint and peanuts. Serve extra peanuts separately, if using.

Useful tip To crack open a coconut, wrap it in a tea towel. Put on a solid base, such as a clean floor, and tap it with a rolling pin.

szechuan bang bang
chicken noodle salad

1 whole small free-range chicken, about 1.5 kg

3 cm fresh ginger, peeled and grated

1 onion, halved

1 tablespoon salt

200 g dried rice vermicelli noodles

20 cm cucumber, peeled and cut into matchstick strips

1 tablespoon pan-toasted sesame seeds, to serve

Chinese sesame dressing

5 tablespoons Chinese sesame paste or smooth peanut butter

2 tablespoons sesame oil

2 tablespoons soy sauce

1 tablespoon chilli sauce

1 tablespoon sugar

½ teaspoon salt

4 tablespoons Chicken Stock (page 62)

Serves 4

Put the chicken into a large saucepan, cover with cold water, then add the ginger, onion and salt. Cover, bring to the boil over medium heat, reduce the heat and simmer for 45 minutes. Let the chicken cool completely in the stock. This may be done a day in advance.

Remove the chicken and drain well, saving the stock for another use. Skin the chicken, take the meat off the bones and shred it finely with a fork. Discard the skin and bones.

Put the noodles into a bowl, cover with boiling water and let soak for 5 minutes. Transfer to a strainer, rinse under cold running water and drain well. Cut the noodles into 3 cm lengths with scissors and transfer to a serving dish. Arrange the cucumber and chicken on top.

Put all the Chinese sesame dressing ingredients into a small bowl, stir well and pour over the chicken. Sprinkle with the toasted sesame seeds, then serve.

The traditional Bang Bang chicken does not include noodles. However, I have included rice vermicelli to make a refreshing salad or one-dish lunch. If you cook it in advance, you will also have excellent chicken stock as a by-product.

Strict Buddhists are vegetarian, so real shark's fin is out of the question. Substituting rice vermicelli noodles seems more ecologically friendly and hurts no one. You don't have to be a Buddhist to enjoy this light but satisfying soup (though Buddhist monks famously enjoy long, healthy lives).

buddhist 'shark's fin' soup

100 g dried rice vermicelli noodles

4 dried shiitake mushrooms

4 dried black Chinese mushrooms

4 dried wood ear mushrooms

1 tablespoon peanut oil

1/2 carrot, cut into matchstick strips

1 leek, thinly sliced

125 g canned bamboo shoots, cut into matchstick strips

125 g Chinese cabbage, thinly shredded

250 g beansprouts

3 tablespoons light soy sauce

1 teaspoon sugar

1/2 teaspoon salt

1/2 teaspoon sesame oil

2 spring onions, finely chopped

1 teaspoon roasted sesame seeds

Serves 4–6

Soak the noodles in boiling water, cover and set aside for 10 minutes or until the noodles have softened. Drain and cut them into 5 cm lengths with scissors.

Put all the dried mushrooms into a bowl and cover with 1 litre boiling water. Let soak until softened, then drain and keep the juice. Cut off all the stems and discard them. Slice the caps thinly.

Heat a wok over high heat and add the peanut oil. Add the mushrooms, carrot, leek, bamboo shoots, cabbage and beansprouts and stir-fry for 5 minutes. Reduce the heat to medium and cook for a further 5 minutes. Add the reserved mushroom juice and bring to the boil.

Add the noodles and reduce the heat to low. Season with soy sauce, sugar and salt. Let simmer for another 5 minutes and turn off the heat.

Ladle into soup bowls, sprinkle with sesame oil, chopped spring onions and sesame seeds, then serve.

soups

2 tablespoons peanut oil

200 g skinless, boneless chicken thighs, thinly sliced

1 onion, thinly sliced lengthways

1 leek, split lengthways, rinsed, well drained and finely chopped

1 carrot, cut into matchstick strips

250 g canned sliced bamboo shoots, rinsed, drained and cut into matchstick strips

16 mangetout, coarsely chopped

250 g beansprouts, rinsed, drained and trimmed

1 teaspoon soy sauce

4 dried ramen noodle nests, 85 g each

sea salt and freshly ground black pepper

Miso soup

1 litre Chicken Stock (page 62)

1 garlic clove, finely chopped

1½ tablespoons mirin (sweetened Japanese rice wine) or dry sherry

4 tablespoons light or medium miso paste

To serve

2 spring onions, finely chopped

1 tablespoon Chilli Oil (page 62)

1 tablespoon sesame seeds, toasted in a dry frying pan

Serves 4

This is a substantial, heart-warming miso soup with a difference from Sapporo, the regional capital of Hokkaido, Japan's northern island. Hokkaido was our equivalent of the 'Wild West frontier' in the mid-19th century, when the new government encouraged large numbers of pioneer farmers and miners to go north in search of a new life.

In the harsh and barren winters, non-traditional ingredients such as garlic and chilli oil warmed the bodies and hearts of the new settlers.

sapporo miso ramen
with chicken

Heat the peanut oil in a wok and swirl to coat. Add the chicken, onion, leek, carrot, bamboo shoots, mangetout and beansprouts and stir-fry over high heat for 5 minutes. Season with the soy sauce, then taste and adjust the seasoning with salt and pepper.

Bring a large saucepan of water to the boil, add the noodles and cook for 2 minutes. Drain and transfer to 4 deep soup bowls.

Meanwhile, put the stock into a saucepan and bring to the boil. Add the garlic, mirin and miso paste. Stir thoroughly to dissolve the paste. Ladle the soup over the noodles and top with the stir-fried mixture.

Sprinkle with the spring onions, chilli oil and sesame seeds and serve immediately.

In Japanese, *kitsune udon*, means 'fox noodles'. Evidently, Japanese foxes love deep-fried tofu, *abura age*. Foxes in Japan are revered messengers of the Shinto gods. A pair of stone carvings of foxes stands guard at the entrances to all Shinto shrines. I never thought this story strange until I came to England, but cultural differences aside, this is a delicious and comforting noodle dish.

4 sheets *abura age* (deep-fried tofu sheets)

8 fresh shiitake mushrooms, stems removed

4 packets (200 g) vacuum-packed fresh udon noodles

4 spring onions, finely chopped

sichimi-tôgarashi (Japanese seven-spice), to serve (optional)

Simmering stock

200 ml Vegetarian Dashi (page 62)

1 tablespoon sugar

1/2 teaspoon mirin (sweetened Japanese rice wine) or dry sherry

2 teaspoons light soy sauce

Noodle broth

1 litre Vegetarian Dashi (page 62)

1 teaspoon salt

1 tablespoon light soy sauce

2 tablespoons mirin (sweetened Japanese rice wine) or dry sherry

Serves 4

fox noodles

To degrease the deep-fried tofu sheets, put them into a sieve and pour boiling water over them. Turn them over and repeat the process. If the tofu sheets are large, the size of a medium brown envelope, cut them into 3 triangles.

To make the simmering stock, put the dashi, sugar, mirin and soy sauce into a saucepan and heat to simmering over medium heat. Add the tofu triangles and shiitake mushrooms. Simmer for 20 minutes or until the stock has almost disappeared. Turn off the heat and let the tofu cool in the saucepan.

Bring a saucepan of water to the boil and cook the noodles for 2 minutes, stirring them with a pair of chopsticks to separate them. Drain and share between 4 individual bowls.

Put the noodle broth ingredients into a saucepan over medium heat – don't let it boil. When hot, ladle the broth over the noodles in the bowls. Arrange the seasoned tofu triangles on top and garnish with the shiitake mushrooms and chopped spring onions. Serve with a small pot of *sichimi-tôgarashi,* if using.

vietnamese
crab noodle soup

400 g dried rice vermicelli noodles

4 tablespoons Asian dried shrimp

2 tablespoons peanut oil

4 shallots, thinly sliced

2 garlic cloves, crushed

2 red chillies, deseeded and finely chopped

4 tomatoes, deseeded and coarsely chopped

200 g cooked white crabmeat, flaked

1.25 litres chicken stock

2 tablespoons Asian fish sauce

1 teaspoon soft brown sugar

1 tablespoon rice vinegar

½ iceberg lettuce, finely sliced

To serve

2 spring onions, finely chopped

a handful of coriander leaves

a handful of mint leaves

1 lime, cut into 4 wedges

Serves 4

This aromatic noodle soup is a speciality of central Vietnam, where all productive land is given over to cultivating rice. The authentic recipe uses tiny freshwater crabs commonly found in paddy fields. Usually they are pounded almost to a paste and made into small dumplings, but this recipe is easier with the crabmeat floating freely in the soup. You don't even have to go crab hunting – I use prepared white crabmeat, fresh or frozen.

Put the noodles into a bowl and cover with boiling water for 10 minutes, or until soft. Drain, rinse under cold running water and drain again. Using kitchen scissors, chop them into manageable lengths, about 5 cm, and set aside.

Put the dried shrimp into another bowl, add 125 ml boiling water and soak for 20 minutes. Drain and reserve the shrimp and their soaking water.

Heat the oil in a wok, swirl to coat, then add the shallots, garlic and chillies. Stir-fry for 1 minute, then add the tomatoes, crabmeat, soaked shrimp, their soaking water and the chicken stock. Season the soup with fish sauce, sugar and vinegar and bring to the boil. Reduce the heat to low and let simmer for 5 minutes.

Turn off the heat and stir in the noodles and lettuce.

Ladle the soup into 4 bowls and serve with the spring onions, coriander and mint leaves and lime wedges on top.

prawn and spinach
wonton noodle soup

200 g fresh or dried egg noodles

1 litre Chicken Stock (page 62)

1 tablespoon soy sauce

100 g Chinese greens such as Chinese cabbage or bok choy, coarsely chopped

sea salt and freshly ground black pepper

2 spring onions, sliced diagonally, to serve

Wontons

2 tablespoons peanut oil

50 g spinach, coarsely chopped

100 g uncooked prawns, peeled, deveined and finely chopped

1 garlic clove, crushed

3 cm fresh ginger, peeled and finely chopped

150 g minced pork

1 egg, separated

20 fresh wonton wrappers

sea salt and freshly ground black pepper

Serves 4

To make the wontons, heat the oil in a wok. Add the spinach and stir-fry over medium heat until soft. Remove from the heat, let cool a little, then squeeze out as much excess juice as possible.

Transfer the spinach to a large bowl, add the prawns, garlic, ginger, minced pork, egg yolk, salt and pepper and mix well.

Put a heaped teaspoon of the pork mixture in the centre of a wonton wrapper. Brush the edges of the wrapper with lightly beaten egg white and fold in half to make a triangle.

Wet the two bottom corners of the triangle and seal them together. (You can prepare up to this point 6 hours in advance and keep the wontons covered and refrigerated.)

Bring a large saucepan of water to the boil, add the fresh noodles, if using, and cook for 2–3 minutes. (If you are using dry noodles, cook for about 3–5 minutes). Scoop out the cooked noodles with a strainer and divide between 4 serving bowls – keep the water simmering.

Put the chicken stock into a second saucepan and heat to simmering – try not to boil or the stock will be cloudy. Season with soy sauce, salt and pepper and keep it simmering.

Return the water to the boil and cook the wontons in batches of 4–5 for 5 minutes each.

Spoon them out and add them to the serving bowls. Using the same boiling water, blanch the Chinese greens for 1 minute, then immediately remove and add to the serving bowls. Ladle the stock into the bowls, top with the spring onions and serve immediately.

This is the Cantonese equivalent of Italian ravioli, though the Chinese would claim that theirs came first. The wonton wrapper is made from egg noodle dough and can be bought fresh or frozen from Chinese shops. The size of wrappers and packets varies, but here I have used twenty of the 7 cm size. Any leftover wrappers can be frozen. Surprisingly easy to make, this simple dish sums up the pure yet comforting Cantonese food that is so rarely seen in restaurants nowadays. It is also a good way of getting children to eat spinach.

spicy chicken noodle soup

2 large chicken thighs, about 400 g

100 g dried beanthread noodles, soaked in boiling water and drained

2 hard-boiled eggs, peeled and halved

100 g fresh beansprouts, rinsed, drained and trimmed

4 sprigs of coriander, coarsely chopped

2 tablespoons crisp deep-fried shallots*

Spice paste

5 cm fresh ginger or galangal, peeled and chopped

4 stalks of lemongrass, outer leaves discarded, remainder finely chopped

8 macadamia nuts

10 garlic cloves, crushed

15 small Thai shallots or 3 regular, coarsely chopped

8 kaffir lime leaves, coarsely chopped

4 tablespoons peanut oil

2 teaspoons ground turmeric

2 tablespoons ground coriander

Serves 4

Available in larger supermarkets or Chinese grocers.

To make the spice paste, all ingredients should be chopped or sliced as much as you can before they are processed. Harder ones such as galangal and lemongrass should be processed until smooth, then the softer ingredients added. Whole dried spices should be ground separately from the 'wet' spices and added later.

Put the chicken into a saucepan, add 1 litre cold water and bring to the boil over medium heat. Reduce the heat and simmer for 1 hour. Remove the chicken from the stock and reserve the stock. Skin the chicken, shred flesh with a fork, then discard the skin and bones.

To make the spice paste, put the ginger, lemongrass and nuts into a blender and work to a smooth paste. Add the garlic, shallots, lime leaves, 2 tablespoons of the peanut oil, the turmeric and coriander and grind again until smooth.

Heat the remaining 2 tablespoons oil in a wok, add 4 tablespoons of the paste (reserving the rest for another use) and stir-fry for 3–4 minutes. Reduce the heat, add the shredded chicken and its stock and simmer for 20 minutes.

Put the drained noodles into 4 deep bowls, then add the halved boiled eggs and beansprouts. Gently ladle in the soup mixture. Sprinkle with the chopped coriander and deep-fried shallots and serve immediately.

Useful tip Any surplus curry paste can be kept refrigerated for 3–4 days or frozen in an ice-cube tray.

The people of Taiwan are as passionate about noodles as the people of mainland China. This is an unusual recipe – for some reason, pumpkins are rarely used in noodle dishes in Asia.

stir-fried clams and pumpkin
with rice stick noodles

4 tablespoons Asian dried shrimp

250 g dried rice stick noodles

4 tablespoons peanut oil

500 g fresh clams, cleaned

250 ml Shaohsing (sweetened Chinese rice wine) or dry sherry

1 teaspoon sesame oil

1 garlic clove, finely crushed

3 cm fresh ginger, peeled and finely grated

250 g fresh pumpkin, peeled, deseeded and cut into tiny wedges or strips

1 tablespoon soy sauce

1/2 teaspoon sugar

sea salt and freshly ground black pepper

4 spring onions, finely chopped, to serve

Serves 4

Put the dried shrimp into a bowl, add 125 ml boiling water and let soak for 15 minutes.

Put the noodles into a second bowl, cover with boiling water and let soak for 5–7 minutes. Drain, rinse under cold running water, drain again and set aside.

Heat 3 tablespoons of the oil in a wok and swirl to coat. Add the clams and stir-fry over high heat, tossing frequently. Add the rice wine, cover with a lid and cook for 2–3 minutes, shaking the wok from time to time. Remove all opened clams with a slotted spoon, discard any that are still closed and reserve the cooking juices. Keep the clams warm in a covered bowl.

Heat the sesame oil and the remaining peanut oil in the wok, add the garlic and ginger and stir-fry for 1 minute. Add the pumpkin, cook for 1 minute, then add the drained shrimp and their soaking water. Add the reserved clam cooking juices and simmer for 5–8 minutes or until the pumpkin is tender.

Add the noodles and toss gently to reheat. Season with soy sauce and sugar, then add salt and pepper to taste.

Serve in 4 heated dishes with the clams and chopped spring onions on top.

fish and seafood

A dish using two kinds of Japanese noodles. Buckwheat soba noodles are robust, no-nonsense everyday fare, while harusame are special – as exquisitely fine and delicate as an April shower: in fact their name means 'spring rain'. If unavailable, use beanthread noodles.

prawn tempura noodles

250 g dried soba noodles

100 g dried harusame noodles, cut into 3 cm lengths

12 king prawns, peeled, deveined and with shallow cuts made across the belly side

1 litre peanut oil or sunflower oil, for deep-frying

Tempura batter

180 ml ice-cold water

1 egg

250 g plain flour, sieved

Dipping sauce

250 ml Dashi (page 62)

1 tablespoon mirin (sweetened Japanese rice wine) or dry sherry

1 tablespoon soy sauce

125 g daikon (mooli or white radish), finely grated

Serves 4

To make the dipping sauce, put the dashi, mirin and soy sauce into a large bowl, add the grated daikon and set aside.

Bring a large saucepan of water to the boil, add the soba noodles and stir with chopsticks. Return to the boil. When the water begins to froth, immediately add a cup of cold water. Return to the boil for the third time, then drain and rinse the noodles under cold running water. You may have to repeat this process, depending on how dry the noodles are. Drain well, pile onto 4 dishes and set aside.

Make the tempura batter just before frying. Put the egg and ice-cold water into a bowl and mix well, then sift the flour over the top. Stir briefly then use immediately.

Fill a wok or saucepan one-third full of oil and heat to 190°C (375°F), or until a piece of noodle fluffs up immediately. Add all the chopped harusame noodles and cook until they turn white and puff up. Scoop out with a slotted spoon and drain on kitchen paper. Reheat the oil, dip the prawns in the batter and gently slide into the oil. Cook for 2–3 minutes or until the batter turns light golden. Drain well on kitchen paper.

Put the harusame on top of the soba noodles and top with the prawns. Serve with the strained dipping sauce.

singapore noodles

250 g thin dried egg noodle nests

2 tablespoons peanut oil

4 shallots, finely chopped

2 garlic cloves, crushed

3 cm fresh ginger,
peeled and grated

200 g canned water chestnuts,
rinsed, drained and
coarsely chopped

200 g pork loin, thinly sliced

400 g uncooked prawns, shelled
and deveined, but tail fins intact

2 eggs, lightly beaten

2 tablespoons soy sauce

2 tablespoons oyster sauce

2 tablespoons Malay mild curry
powder (optional)

sea salt and freshly
ground black pepper

To serve

2 spring onions, finely chopped

1 tablespoon crisp deep-fried
onions*

125 ml Chilli Dipping Sauce
(page 62)

Serves 4

*Available in larger supermarkets
or Chinese grocers.*

This is one of those national dishes that is better known outside its country of origin. But it is simple and, above all, versatile – as soon as you understand its basic principle, you can improvise according to whatever you have in your storecupboard or refrigerator.

Bring a large saucepan of water to the boil, add the egg noodle nests and cook for 3 minutes, gently stirring with chopsticks to separate the noodles. Do not overcook them because they will be stir-fried later. Rinse in cold running water, drain well and set aside.

Heat the oil in a wok and swirl to coat. Add the shallots, garlic and grated ginger and stir-fry for 2 minutes. Add the water chestnuts, pork and prawns and stir-fry for a further 3 minutes.

Add the beaten eggs and swirl to coat the wok. Cook for 1 minute.

Add the cooked noodles and toss lightly to mix with the other ingredients. Season with soy sauce and oyster sauce. Turn off the heat, stir in the curry powder, if using, then add salt and pepper to taste.

Top with the spring onions and crisp deep-fried onions and serve with a separate dish of Chilli Dipping Sauce.

200 g dried rice vermicelli noodles

750 g oily white fish cutlets, such as swordfish or yellowtail tuna

2 stalks of lemongrass, bruised

3 cm fresh ginger, cut into 4 slices

2 onions, halved

1 red chilli, halved lengthways

2 tablespoons fish sauce

3 tablespoons peanut oil

½ Chinese cabbage, finely sliced

3 tablespoons rice flour

500 ml coconut milk

about 1 teaspoon sugar

about 1 teaspoon salt

Curry paste

2 onions, coarsely chopped

4 garlic cloves, crushed

2 cm fresh ginger, peeled and grated

1 stalk of lemongrass, outer leaves discarded, remainder very finely chopped

1 red chilli, deseeded and chopped

1 teaspoon shrimp paste

2 teaspoons ground cumin

2 teaspoons ground turmeric

1 teaspoon ground coriander

To serve

lime wedges

deep-fried onions (page 38)

chilli flakes

Serves 4

burmese **fish curry noodles**

Even if you know nothing else about Burmese food, you may still be familiar with this dish. Like Burma itself, this robust, aromatic curry draws heavily on the food culture of both India and South-east Asia. Any leftover curry paste can be frozen in an ice-cube tray.

Put the noodles into a bowl, cover with boiling water and let soak for 15 minutes. Drain, then add to a saucepan of boiling water and cook for 1 minute. Drain and keep the noodles warm.

Put the fish into a saucepan and cover with cold water. Add the lemongrass, ginger, onions, red chilli and fish sauce. Bring to the boil over medium heat, then reduce the heat and simmer for 10 minutes. Remove the fish from the heat and set it aside. Strain the cooking liquid into a bowl and reserve.

To make the curry paste, use a mortar and pestle to pound the onions, garlic, ginger, lemongrass and chilli to a smooth paste. Add the shrimp paste, cumin, turmeric and ground coriander and mix well.

Heat the oil in a wok and swirl to coat. Add the curry paste and cook for 5 minutes until aromatic.

Add the reserved fish to the wok, then add the cabbage and 1 litre of the reserved fish stock. Bring to the boil, then reduce the heat and simmer for 5 minutes. Put the rice flour into a small bowl, add little water and stir to dissolve. Add to the curry, then add the coconut milk and stir until thickened. Simmer for 5 minutes, then add sugar and salt to taste.

Put the cooked noodles into a large bowl and ladle the curry on top. Serve with lime wedges, deep-fried onions and chilli flakes.

Probably the most popular of all the classic Thai stir-fry noodle dishes. It is quick and easy to make, just delicate noodles twisted around plump prawns and crunchy beansprouts. It is positively jumping with flavours.

200 g dried flat rice stick noodles

4 tablespoons peanut oil

2 shallots, finely chopped

200 g peeled uncooked prawns, deveined

2 garlic cloves, crushed

2 large eggs, lightly beaten

200 g beansprouts, rinsed, drained and trimmed

2 tablespoons dried shrimps, ground to powder in with a mortar and pestle

Spicy seasoning sauce

2 tablespoons Thai fish sauce

2 tablespoons tomato ketchup

1 tablespoon lime juice

1 tablespoon palm sugar or soft light brown sugar

To serve

1 tablespoon dried red chilli flakes

2 spring onions, finely chopped

2 tablespoons coarsely chopped coriander leaves

1 lime, cut into 4 wedges

Serves 4

pad thai
thai fried noodles

Put the noodles into a bowl, cover with hot water and let soak for 10–15 minutes until softened. Rinse in cold water, drain well and set aside.

To make the spicy seasoning sauce, put all the ingredients into a bowl and mix well.

Heat the oil in a wok and swirl to coat. Add the shallots and stir-fry for about 2 minutes or until soft and golden. Add the prawns and garlic and stir-fry for 3 minutes. Add the egg and cook until softly set, stirring with chopsticks to scramble.

Reduce the heat slightly and add the drained noodles. Add half the beansprouts and half the ground shrimp and toss well.

Pour the spicy sauce mixture around the edge of the wok and turn off the heat immediately. Stir well to ensure the noodle mixture is well coated with the sauce. Sprinkle with the remaining beansprouts and ground shrimps, then add the chilli flakes, spring onions and coriander leaves. Serve in bowls with a lime wedge for squeezing.

marinated duck breast
with soba noodles

2 duck breasts, 200 g each

400 g dried soba noodles

Marinade

600 ml Dashi (page 62)

4 tablespoons soy sauce

3 tablespoons sake

2 tablespoons mirin (sweetened
Japanese rice wine) or dry sherry

Dipping sauce

250 ml Dashi (page 62)

1 tablespoon soy sauce

1 tablespoon mirin (sweetened
Japanese rice wine) or dry sherry

To serve

2 spring onions, finely chopped

2 tablespoons wasabi powder,
dissolved with 1 tablespoon
water into a paste

Serves 4

Trim excess fat from the edges of the duck breasts and prick the
skin with a fork.

Heat a frying pan over medium heat. Add the breasts skin side
down and cook for 8–10 minutes or until the skin is crisp and
golden. Drain off the fat. Turn them over to cook the other side
for 2–3 minutes.

Remove the breasts and plunge them into a bowl of hot water
to wash off the fat.

Put the marinade ingredients into a bowl and stir well. Add the
cooked breasts and set aside in the refrigerator for at least
3 hours or overnight.

When ready to serve, remove the breasts and cut them into thin
slices, about 2–3 mm wide. Mix the dipping sauce ingredients in
a small bowl and serve in 4 dipping bowls.

Bring a saucepan of water to the boil, add the soba noodles and
when the water is about to boil over, pour in a cup of cold water
and return to the boil. You may have to repeat this once more,
depending on how dry the noodles are. Drain and rinse the
noodles under cold running water. Drain well again.

Put the noodles onto 4 heated plates and arrange the duck slices
on top. Sprinkle the chopped spring onions over the top and put
a small mound of wasabi paste beside them. Serve the dipping
sauce separately.

meat and poultry

This is a popular northern Thai curried noodle soup with crisp, deep-fried wheat noodles and is very like the traditional curry noodles of neighbouring Burma.

chiang mai chicken noodles

500 ml peanut oil, for deep-frying

400 g fresh egg noodles, or 200 g dried noodles

2 tablespoons Thai red curry paste

1 teaspoon ground turmeric

1 teaspoon ground cumin

4 boneless chicken thighs, coarsely chopped

250 ml Chicken Stock (page 62)

250 ml canned coconut milk

1 tablespoon Thai fish sauce

4 spring onions, finely chopped

4 tablespoons coarsely chopped coriander leaves

To serve

4 pink Thai shallots, thinly sliced

2 limes, halved

1 tablespoon crushed dried red chillies

Serves 4

Put the peanut oil into a wok and heat until a piece of noodle will fluff up immediately. Add half the noodles and deep-fry for 2 minutes or until gold and crisp. Remove and drain on kitchen paper and set aside. Drain the oil into a heatproof container and let cool.

Meanwhile bring a saucepan of water to the boil, add the remaining noodles, stir with chopsticks and cook for 1 minute. Remove, drain and rinse under cold running water. Drain well and set aside.

Take 2 tablespoons of the reserved oil and heat in the wok. Add the curry paste, turmeric and cumin and stir-fry for 2 minutes.

Add the chicken and stir-fry for a further 3 minutes. Add the chicken stock and bring to the boil. Reduce the heat, then add the coconut milk and fish sauce. Simmer for about 10–15 minutes, then turn off the heat and stir in the spring onions and coriander.

Pour boiling water onto the cooked noodles to reheat, drain and transfer to 4 large bowls. Ladle the soup over the top, add the deep-fried noodles and serve with shallots, limes and dried chillies.

Note Fresh noodles are best for this recipe, but if unavailable, use dried. Dried noodles take slightly longer to boil and fry.

vietnamese chicken noodle **pho**

1 whole small free-range chicken, about 1.5 kg

1 tablespoon salt

2 red onions, halved

3 cm fresh ginger, thickly sliced

1 cinnamon stick

1 whole star anise

4 cardamom pods, crushed

2 kaffir lime leaves, roughly torn

2 teaspoons brown sugar

4 tablespoons fish sauce

250 g fresh rice noodles

sea salt and freshly ground black pepper

4 tablespoons crisp deep-fried shallots, to serve*

Table salad

200 g fresh beansprouts, rinsed, drained and trimmed

a handful of fresh mint

a handful of Thai basil

a handful of coriander leaves

2 spring onions, chopped

2 fresh red chillies, finely chopped

1 lime, cut into 4 wedges

Serves 4

Available in larger supermarkets or Chinese grocers.

This is a chicken version of the famous Vietnamese beef noodle soup, *pho bo*. Yet it is every bit as full of complex flavours and is as satisfying, but lighter and perhaps more subtle than the beef version. I prefer to use a whole chicken – you get plenty of superb chicken stock and have cooked chicken left for another meal or two. However, if you are making this dish for only one or two people, use one chicken leg and reduce the quantity of other ingredients accordingly. Whatever the quantity, it is the quality of chicken that is important and determines the flavour of the soup.

Put the chicken into a large saucepan, then add the salt, onions, ginger, cinnamon stick, star anise, cardamom pods and lime leaves. Add 3 litres water and bring to the boil over medium heat and skim off the foam. Reduce the heat to low and let simmer for 3–6 hours. Remove the chicken from the pan and strain the stock through a fine sieve into a bowl. Reserve the chicken, keeping it warm in a low oven.

Ladle 1 litre of the stock into a saucepan and season with sugar and fish sauce. Taste and adjust the seasoning with salt and pepper.

Put the rice noodles into a bowl, cover with boiling water and stir gently with chopsticks to separate. Drain immediately and pour into 4 large soup bowls.

Shred the meat from the chicken thighs and breasts with a fork. Put the shredded chicken on top of the noodles and ladle in the hot soup. Sprinkle with deep-fried shallots.

Serve with a plate of table salad – beansprouts, herbs, spring onions, chillies and lime wedges for each person to add according to taste.

shanghai pork noodles

400 g dried rice vermicelli
or rice stick noodles

4 dried shiitake mushrooms

2 tablespoons dried shrimps

4 tablespoons peanut oil

1 garlic clove, finely crushed

3 cm fresh ginger,
peeled and grated

50 g pork fillet, cut into
matchstick strips

50 g carrots, cut into
matchstick strips

50 g canned bamboo shoots,
cut into matchstick strips
(or baby corn)

50 g mangetout, cut into
matchstick strips

2 tablespoons soy sauce

sea salt and freshly
ground black pepper

2 spring onions,
finely chopped, to serve

Serves 4

I have tried so many times to make this recipe more sophisticated, elaborate and complicated but no matter what I have tried, it still remains the simplest, easiest and quickest foolproof stir-fry.

Put the noodles into a large bowl, add boiling water to cover and let soak for 15 minutes. Drain, rinse under cold running water and drain again.

Put the shiitake mushrooms into a bowl, add 125 ml boiling water and let soak for 10 minutes. Drain, but keep the soaking water. Remove and discard the stems and slice the caps thinly.

Put the dried shrimps into a bowl, add 125 ml boiling water and soak for 10 minutes. Drain, but keep the soaking water.

Heat the oil in a wok and swirl to coat. Add the garlic, ginger, pork, mushrooms, shrimps, carrot, bamboo shoots and mangetout and stir-fry for 5 minutes or until all are cooked.

Add the noodles and the reserved soaking water from the mushrooms and shrimp. Season with soy sauce, salt and pepper. Stir well and let the noodles soak up the juices.

sukiyaki

500 g top-quality sirloin beef,
cut into 3 mm slices

1 tablespoon sake

1 packet fresh shirataki noodles,
about 200 g, drained

2 large white onions,
cut into 8 wedges

8 baby leeks, chopped
into 3 cm lengths

200 g Chinese greens, such as
baby bok choy, shungiku or
mituba, coarsely chopped

8 fresh shiitake mushrooms,
stems discarded

1 block firm tofu, well drained and
cut into 3 cm cubes

4 fresh free-range eggs, lightly
beaten (optional), to serve

1 tablespoon peanut oil,
for brushing

**Kansai-style wari-shita
cooking sauce**

250 ml soy sauce

250 g sugar

250 ml mirin (sweet Japanese
rice wine) or dry sherry

*a tabletop grill or heavy
cast-iron grill pan with
separate table burner*

Serves 4

This is an easy dish to prepare – the equivalent of Japanese fondue. You arrange all the sliced ingredients on a large platter and you and your guests cook everything at the table – fun for even the most reluctant cook. The traditional dipping sauce is beaten raw egg – I never much cared for it, but I shall leave you to decide.

Arrange the beef slices on a large plate, sprinkle with sake and set aside. Put the shirataki noodles into a bowl, cover with boiling water and let soak for 2 minutes. Drain and rinse under cold running water. Drain well, chop coarsely and add to a serving platter or put into small bowls. Arrange the onion wedges, baby leeks, greens, shiitake mushrooms and tofu cubes on the platter.

To make the wari-shita cooking sauce, put all the ingredients into a jug and stir until the sugar has dissolved. Set aside.

Set the table-top grill on a heatproof surface in the middle of the table, preheat its pan according to the manufacturer's instructions and seat your guests. Brush the grill pan with the oil, add the onion wedges and baby leeks and stir-fry for 2 minutes or until soft. Put the beaten eggs, if using, into 4 dipping bowls, one for each guest.

Pour half the cooking sauce into the pan. When the liquid begins to bubble, add half the remaining vegetables, leaving some space for the beef. Cook 1 beef slice per guest at a time and, as the beef changes colour, invite your guests to serve themselves from the pan.

Let the guests cook more beef and vegetables themselves. Add more of the cooking sauce to top up the liquid level in the pan.

jap chae korean noodles

200 g dried Korean vermicelli
noodles (see recipe introduction)

2 dried Chinese black mushrooms

3 tablespoons peanut oil

1 large onion, coarsely chopped

3 garlic cloves, crushed

3 cm fresh ginger, peeled and
finely grated

200 g sirloin steak, thinly sliced

1 carrot, cut into matchstick strips

1 green pepper, deseeded and cut
into matchstick strips

a bunch of Chinese garlic chives,
chopped coarsely

2 teaspoons sugar

½ teaspoon salt

2 tablespoons soy sauce

1 teaspoon sesame oil

To serve

2 spring onions, finely chopped
diagonally

2 tablespoons
toasted sesame seeds

Chilli Dipping Sauce (page 62)

500 g fresh or canned Korean
kimchi pickle (optional)

Serves 4

This Korean national dish is eaten for breakfast, lunch or a one-dish supper – in other words, all the time. Korean vermicelli noodles, made from sweet potato, have a more resilient texture than the Chinese version. If unavailable, use any rice vermicelli or beanthread noodles instead. Serve warm with Chilli Dipping Sauce and, of course, the nation's favourite – kimchi pickle, if available.

Bring a saucepan of water to the boil, then add the noodles and stir. Reduce the heat to medium and cook for 3 minutes – do not overcook the noodles. Drain and rinse under cold running water. Drain again and set aside.

Put the mushrooms into a bowl, add 250 ml boiling water and soak for 20 minutes or until soft. Drain and slice thinly.

Heat the oil in a wok and swirl to coat. Add the onion and stir-fry over moderate heat for 3 minutes. Add the garlic, ginger and steak and stir-fry for a further 2 minutes.

Add the carrot, green pepper, mushrooms and Chinese garlic chives and stir-fry for 2 minutes. Turn off the heat. Season with sugar, salt, soy sauce and sesame oil and mix well. Turn the heat back on for 1 minute, fold in the noodles and stir gently.

Ladle into 4 dishes and top with spring onions and sesame seeds. Serve with Chilli Dipping Sauce, and a bowl of kimchi, if using.

300 g dried Korean naeng myun noodles or Japanese soba noodles

1 tablespoon sesame oil

200 g daikon (mooli or white radish), peeled and finely grated

1 teaspoon red chilli powder

2 tablespoons rice vinegar or cider vinegar

1 teaspoon sugar

1/2 teaspoon salt

2 baby cucumbers, peeled and cut into 5 cm matchstick strips

1 crisp Japanese nashi pear or other firm pear, peeled and cut into 5 cm matchstick strips

Seasoning paste

4 garlic cloves, crushed

2 tablespoons hot chilli paste

2 tablespoons sugar

2 teaspoons sesame oil

1 tablespoon sesame seeds, toasted in a dry frying pan

Spicy beef

2 tablespoons peanut oil

2 garlic cloves, well crushed

400 g sirloin steak, sliced into thin strips

2 tablespoons soy sauce

1 tablespoon sugar

2 spring onions, finely chopped

1/2 teaspoon ground black pepper

1–2 tablespoons red chilli paste

Serves 4

korean beef
with cold buckwheat noodles

Naeng myun means 'cold noodle' – indeed, my first encounter with this dish was on a hot summer's day in Seoul. I was quite revived by its punchy flavours and amazing combinations of crunchy textures. Naeng myun are Korea's answer to soba noodles, but are chewier and have a lighter, more translucent appearance. The dried variety can be found in Korean or some other Asian shops, but soba noodles can be used instead.

Bring a large saucepan of water to the boil, add the noodles and cook until the foam begins to rise. Add a cup of cold water and let the water return to the boil (you may have to repeat this until the noodles are cooked *al dente*). Stir with a chopstick to separate them. Drain and rinse in cold water to remove the starch, then drain again. Stir in the sesame oil to stop the noodles from sticking together, then cover and refrigerate.

To prepare the beef, heat the oil in a wok, add all the ingredients for the spicy beef and stir-fry for 3 minutes. Set aside.

Put the grated daikon into a bowl and stir in the chilli powder, vinegar and sugar. Set aside.

Sprinkle salt onto the cucumber strips and leave for 10 minutes. Drain and pat them dry with kitchen paper.

Put all the seasoning paste ingredients into a bowl and mix well.

Put the noodles, daikon mixture, cucumbers, pear and beef into a large bowl and toss well. Serve with a dish of seasoning paste.

No matter how often I make this dish, each time I still get a childish excitement when the fine vermicelli noodles puff up in the oil and turn into a beautiful sculpture. It makes you feel like a wizard in the kitchen. You may vary the ingredients according to taste and season. Spectacular and deliciously crunchy.

1 litre peanut oil, for deep-frying

125 g thin dried rice vermicelli noodles

6 shallots, thinly sliced

2 garlic cloves, finely crushed

1 large red chilli, deseeded and finely chopped

300 g minced chicken

150 g uncooked peeled prawns, finely chopped

100 g fresh beansprouts, rinsed, drained and trimmed

2 tablespoons palm sugar or light brown sugar

2 tablespoons Thai fish sauce

2 tablespoons rice vinegar

freshly squeezed juice of 1 lime

To serve

1–2 red chillies, finely chopped

4 tablespoons coarsely chopped coriander leaves

4 spring onions, chopped

Serves 4

thai mee krob
with stir-fried pork and chicken

Fill a wok or deep-fat fryer one-third full of oil, or to the manufacturer's recommended level. Heat the oil to 180°C (350°F) or until a piece of noodle fluffs up immediately. Cut the noodles into short, manageable lengths with scissors. Cook a small bundle of noodles at a time – they take only a matter of seconds to puff up and turn golden, so if you cook them a few at a time, they won't be overcooked.

As each bundle is cooked, remove and drain on kitchen paper. Keep them warm in a low oven while you cook the remainder.

Heat 1 tablespoon of the oil in a second wok, add the shallots and stir-fry for 2–3 minutes. Add the garlic, chilli, chicken, prawns and beansprouts and toss for a further 3 minutes.

Reduce the heat and season with sugar, fish sauce and vinegar and mix well. Turn off the heat and add the lime juice.

Put two-thirds of the noodles onto a large heated serving dish. Add the cooked mixture, then the chopped chillies, coriander and spring onions and top with the remainder of the noodles and serve. Alternatively, serve on 4 separate dishes.

pancit canton

200 g thick dried egg noodles

1 tablespoon sesame oil

4 tablespoons peanut oil

1 onion, thinly sliced

2 garlic cloves, finely crushed

100 g streaky bacon,
finely chopped

200 g spring cabbage,
thinly sliced

1 carrot, cut into matchstick strips

1 celery stalk, cut into
matchstick strips

100 g fresh beansprouts, rinsed,
drained and trimmed

½ teaspoon salt

1 teaspoon sugar

1 tablespoon soy sauce,
plus extra to serve

1 tablespoon oyster sauce

a pinch of freshly ground pepper

250 ml Chicken Stock (page 62)

chilli sauce, to serve

Serves 4

Pancit Canton simply means 'Chinese noodles' in the Philippines. My children were brought up on this dish whenever I was off duty in the kitchen. It is simple – just a Filipino adaptation of chow mein. You may, and should, improvise with whatever you can find in your refrigerator.

Bring a large saucepan of water to the boil, add the noodles and cook for 2 minutes, gently stirring with chopsticks to separate them.

Drain, rinse under cold running water and drain again. Transfer to a bowl, sprinkle with the sesame oil and stir briefly to keep the noodles separate. Set aside.

Heat 2 tablespoons of the peanut oil in a wok, add the onion, garlic, bacon, cabbage, carrot, celery and beansprouts and stir-fry for 3–5 minutes.

Season the mixture with salt, sugar, soy sauce, oyster sauce and pepper. Transfer the mixture to a bowl and set aside. Wipe the wok clean with kitchen paper.

Heat the remaining oil in the wok, add the noodles, toss for 1 minute, then add the chicken stock. Bring to the boil and when the liquid is reduced to about half, add the stir-fry mixture and mix well for 2 minutes. Taste and adjust the seasoning with soy sauce, salt and pepper.

Serve in 4 heated dishes, with extra soy sauce or chilli sauce served separately.

sauces and stocks

sweet chilli dipping sauce

Sweeter, less salty and less sharp than chilli dipping sauce.

250 g fresh chillies, deseeded

4 garlic cloves, crushed

1 teaspoon salt

100 g palm or light brown sugar

125 ml water

Put the chillies into a saucepan, add 100 ml water and cook until soft. Blend with the remaining ingredients, then return to the saucepan and cook over low heat for 10–15 minutes. Let cool, then store in an airtight container in the refrigerator. It
will keep for 4 weeks.

nuóc cham dipping sauce

The classic Vietnamese dipping sauce. Vegetarians use light soy sauce instead of fish sauce. It must be used the day it's made.

1 tablespoon sugar

1 teaspoon rice vinegar

1 red bird's eye chilli, finely chopped

2 garlic cloves, finely crushed

1 tablespoon lime juice

2 tablespoons fish sauce

Heat 50 ml water in a small saucepan, add the sugar and vinegar and stir to dissolve the sugar. Let cool, then add the remaining ingredients.

spicy soy vinaigrette dip

A dipping sauce with more depth and flavour than soy and rice vinegar. Good with deep-fried dishes.

100 ml soy sauce

1 tablespoon Chilli Dipping Sauce

freshly squeezed juice of 1 lime or ½ lemon

2 tablespoons rice vinegar

Mix all the ingredients in a screw-top jar and shake well. Refrigerate for up to 1 week.

asian pesto

Toss through any plain fresh hot noodles, just like an Italian pesto. It doesn't keep, so use immediately to capture the fresh herbal flavours.

50 g roasted unsalted peanuts

100 g fresh coriander leaves, including some stems, coarsely chopped

50 g fresh Thai or sweet basil leaves, coarsely chopped

50 g fresh mint leaves, coarsely chopped

4 spring onions, coarsely chopped including green parts

grated zest and juice of 2 unwaxed limes

75 ml canned coconut milk

1 large green chilli, deseeded

1 large garlic clove, crushed

1 teaspoon sugar

1 teaspoon salt

1 teaspoon freshly ground green or white pepper

Put all the ingredients into a blender or food processor and grind to a smooth paste.

dashi

Dashi is the basic Japanese stock. Quick and easy to make, it appears in almost every aspect of Japanese cooking.

postcard-sized piece of konbu (dried kelp)

25 g dried bonito fish flakes

Wipe the konbu with a damp cloth. Put into a saucepan and add 1 litre cold water. Bring to the boil over medium heat and remove the konbu just before the water starts to boil. Let the water boil for a minute, then turn off the heat. Add the bonito flakes and let them settle to the bottom.

Strain the stock through a muslin-lined sieve. Dashi does not keep, so use it the same day.

For vegetarian dashi, omit the bonito and double the quantity of konbu.

chicken stock

1 kg chicken bones, necks and wings

1 onion, unpeeled and halved

3 cm fresh ginger, thickly sliced

2 garlic cloves, crushed

1 teaspoon salt

Wash the chicken bones and put into a large heavy-based saucepan. Add the other ingredients and cover with 2–3 litres cold water. Bring to the boil over medium heat. Skim off any froth that rises to the surface. Reduce the heat and simmer for 3 hours. Let cool, then strain through a fine-meshed sieve. The stock can be refrigerated for 5 days or frozen in ice-cube trays.

chilli oil

I prefer to make my own chilli oil – the flavour is better than shop-bought ones and it is much more economical. A few drops go a long way. It will keep almost indefinitely in a screw-top bottle stored in a cool, dark place.

200 ml peanut oil

50 ml sesame oil

4 tablespoons dried red chilli flakes

1 teaspoon black peppercorns

Heat both oils in a wok over high heat until almost smoking. Add the chilli flakes and peppercorns. Remove from the heat and let cool. Strain through a fine sieve into a screw-top bottle.

chilli dipping sauce

The level of heat of this dipping sauce depends on the chillies you choose. I use large chillies, with a heat level that's easier to control than the small Thai varieties.

250 g fresh chillies, deseeded

4 garlic cloves, crushed

2 tablespoons coarsely chopped fresh ginger

4 tablespoons soy sauce

2 tablespoons sugar

1 teaspoon salt

150 ml rice vinegar

Put the chillies into a saucepan and cover with water. Cook over medium heat until soft. Drain and transfer to a blender. Add all the other ingredients and blend to a smooth paste. Transfer the mixture back to the saucepan and cook over low heat for 10–15 minutes. Let cool, then store in an airtight container in the refrigerator. It will keep for 4 weeks.

index